Down in the

Down in the woods
on Saturday,
story-book people
have come to play.

Little Bo-Peep's there
with her sheep.

Little Boy Blue's
fast asleep.

Miss Muffet's eating
her curds and whey.

Red Riding Hood's there
on her skateboard today.

Goldilocks plays
with Baby Bear.

Even Humpty Dumpty's there.

Their favourite game
is hide-and-seek.
Red Riding Hood's
careful not to peek.

Where are they hiding?
Where can they be?

Start looking, Red Riding Hood.
Who can you see?

Somebody's hiding
behind a wall.

Oh, Humpty! Watch out!
Or you will fall.

There's a bowl
beside a tuffet.

I know who.
It's Little Miss Muffet.

Someone's asleep,
and there are some sheep.

It's Little Boy Blue
and Little Bo-Peep.

And who's that wearing
spotted socks?

It's not Baby Bear,
but Goldilocks.

No one's left hiding
in the woods.
They've all been found.
Isn't that good?

Down in the woods
on Saturday,
story-book people
go home from play!